KICKBACK

Confessions of a Mortgage Salesman

By Ted Janusz

Insight Publishing

Sevierville, Tennessee

KICKBACK
Confessions of a Mortgage Salesman

This book is available at quantity discounts for bulk purchases. For information, please phone (888) 267-2665

Ted Janusz is available to speak at your next event. For information, please phone (800) 987-7771 or visit www.bookaspeaker.com.

Published by Insight Publishing Company
P. O. Box 4189
Sevierville, Tennessee 37864

Many thanks to Production Manager Tennille Crump, Graphic Designer Julie Whitaker, Sandra Pinkoski, editor, and my lovely wife Luanne for their contributions to this project.

Printed in The United States
ISBN: 1-60013-001-1

Table Of Contents

Introduction

I confess. I stole thousands of dollars. Maybe even thousands of *your* dollars. Oh, I was never tried and put in prison for it. What I did was perfectly legal. And it is done every day in professional-looking offices all across the country.

But let me explain. I was a mortgage loan officer. (Actually, a *senior* loan officer.) You'd know my mortgage company. They advertise a lot—on the radio, billboards, and telephone directory covers. The same places the "ambulance-chaser" lawyers advertise. Looking for the naïve, unsophisticated buyers.

Many of my clients needlessly paid me thousands of extra dollars in fees on their mortgages and refinancing transactions.

I no longer am in the mortgage business.

By your reading this book, it is my hope that you can save hundreds or even thousands of dollars on your next mortgage or refinance transaction. I hope, by this book, to pay back at least *some* of the money I stole.

Chapter Nine

How the Lender Can Make Money on You

The lender can make money on you in three ways:

1. **Interest rate** — If the lender is lending you his or her own money, the lender makes money on you every month. Jimmy Stewart portrayed this kind of banker, known as a "portfolio" lender, in the perennial holiday classic movie "It's a Wonderful Life." But portfolio lenders are becoming more and more rare. Although some credit unions and others may have a pool of funds available to loan, most lenders get their funds from other sources which we will discuss later. Did you ever wonder how a business that operates out of nothing more than a hut is able to loan hundreds of thousands of dollars? It's because it's not *their* money!

2. **Origination fee** — also known as "points." One point equals one percent of the loan. The origination fee is simply a *commission*. This is the fee the lender charges for the services of shuffling money

from the secondary lender — the source of the funds — to you.

3. **Service release premium** — As discussed earlier, this is the "kickback" fee that may be paid to the lender, maybe even without his knowledge, by Mr. LTP. The SRP is a "back-end" fee the secondary supplier of the mortgage funds sometimes pays the primary lender for "upselling" the rate. Mr. LTP could have been extended a mortgage at the "less-than-perfect" rate of nine percent, but we stuck him with an eleven percent rate. In the process, we as the lender earned several thousand dollars from the supplier of the funds. This is in addition to the "front-end" origination fee.

How quickly these fees can add up!

Chapter Ten

What is the "Right" Origination Fee?

L ike most of the charges we will discuss, the origination fee is *negotiable*. But most loan officers wouldn't want you to believe that.

The origination fee could be four percent or two percent or one percent or . . . even *nothing at all*!

The highest-earning loan officer at our company would refuse to do a deal with anything less that a two percent origination fee. "It's standard," she would scoff if anyone would dare to challenge her.

This would mean that her commission on a $200,000 mortgage would be a *minimum* of $4,000. Although she would need to share that fee with the company, it may be only one of several loans she would write that day. And this was just the *first* fee on the mortgage.

You may say, "But on my last mortgage, I don't remember writing a check for $4,000."

That's because the origination fee can be incorporated into the loan.

For example, say you were planning on taking out a mortgage for $100,000. But now the total will be at least $104,000. This means you will be paying the principal (and interest) on a significantly higher loan amount.

Or, another way of looking at the situation is that you have just lost $4,000 in equity in your house. When you sell your house, you will automatically reduce your proceeds by four grand.

This makes diligently clipping coupons to save a dollar each at the grocery store seem kind of meaningless by comparison, doesn't it?

On my last mortgage (obtained from a bank, *not* my former mortgage company), I paid *no* origination fee. *You* can, too!

Chapter Eleven

Who has the Advantage—
You or the Mortgage Lender?

W hat would be my chances of making a trip to Las Vegas once or twice a year and beating the odds to reap a big payoff? Especially when I would be going up against blackjack dealers and casino owners who make a great living doing what they do every day?

Or what are the chances of striking a great deal against an automotive dealership when I go to buy a new car once every half-dozen years, especially when the dealership negotiates with (and wins against) all kinds of customers each day? (And how many new car dealerships do you see go out of business? In good times and in bad, they *know* what they need to do to thrive in business.)

I had to laugh. Yesterday, after a seminar, I drove past a casino in Louisiana that had in front of it, overlooking the interstate, a big billboard with a photograph of an attractive woman. Underneath the photo was the promise: Our slots are looser than a hug from your ex-girlfriend.

Even though the casinos and car dealers might try to entice me with signs about "loose slots" or "below invoice" sales, these establishments know their businesses well enough to *never* lose their shirts — far better than I will *ever* know their businesses.

The average American moves once every seven years. Many of these moves include a new mortgage. That mortgage will pay for the most expensive asset you are ever likely to own. Continue to read this book and we'll show you how you can put the odds in your favor.

Chapter Twelve

How Most People Shop for a Mortgage

"What is your rate?" the first caller would ask me. He thought of himself as a savvy mortgage shopper, so he was calling a number of mortgage companies trying to secure the best rate.

He would expect me to reply with a response of six percent or five and three-quarters percent or six and one-half percent so that he would be able to compare it to the other responses he had already received.

Instead I would simply reply, "What rate would you like?"

Silence.

You've probably seen or heard advertisements that scream an enticing four percent mortgage (or an even lower rate). The ads can be true. Such mortgages are available—for a price. What would you willing to pay in additional closing costs to get a below-market rate?

Caller number two is now on the line. "I'm interested in that five and one-half percent mortgage I saw advertised in the paper."

If the rate was quoted in the Sunday paper, the ad was probably composed on Thursday or Friday. It is now Monday.

Stock prices change at least daily. So do mortgage interest rates. Imagine calling your broker and asking to buy stock at a price you saw in the newspaper late last week.

My boss, Mr. T-N-T, told me that my goal was to give each caller *just enough* information to get them in the door. No more. Why?

It is very difficult to sell anyone anything over the phone. But, if you can get the potential customer to come into the office, bear his or her personal and financial soul, and then the two of you labor together to complete those extensive and tedious forms — well, Mr. T-N-T would know you've got 'em!

Chapter Thirteen

Where is the Best
Place to get a Mortgage?

Mortgage lenders fall into three general categories:

Banks—Some banks are "portfolio" lenders, meaning that they loan their own money. The bank officers may get together once or twice a month to set rates and other lending terms as well as to approve mortgage applications. But most banks do not loan their own money. In fact, they might not even service your loan after they secure it.

Mortgage brokers—They bring the buyer (you) and the seller (the secondary lender) together. For that service, they will earn a fee.

Mortgage bankers—A hybrid of the above two sources. They may make mortgages available to you through a line of business credit they possess. Then they will quickly sell off your loan to allow them to write new mortgage business.

WHERE SHOULD YOU TRY FIRST?

Talk to a mortgage broker or banker you *know* you can trust.

If you don't know one, maybe a friend, relative, or your Realtor can recommend one. If you don't have such a friend in the business, I would suggest a bank.

Banks are usually more regulated than the other two options on the number and amount of fees they can charge.

A potential drawback to dealing with a bank, though, is that the bank may charge a mortgage application fee.

Q: Why do banks charge an application fee?

A: Banks generally only want to deal with the best borrowers—those with the highest credit worthiness. They don't want to put up with the borrower with the spaghetti-stained W-2 forms. Banks know that by charging an up-front fee they can often dissuade those with "less than perfect" credit who won't want to take a chance on being rejected from applying. However, if you are approved for a mortgage, the bank will often apply the application fee to the cost of the appraisal.

Chapter Fourteen

How to Take the Advantage the Lender has Over You

D r. Stephen R. Covey's critically acclaimed *The 7 Habits of Highly Effective People* are meant to be applied to all areas of life to help ensure one's success. Let's examine how you are using some of them to benefit yourself in the mortgage application process:

- **Habit 1: Be Proactive** — You are already taking the initiative by reading this book, putting you miles ahead of the typical uninformed applicant.
- **Habit 2: Begin With the End in Mind** — Mortgage planning is just a small part (although a highly critical component) of your overall financial plan. In this case, ask yourself, "How long am I likely to occupy the house? Fifteen years? Thirty years, or less than seven years?" Your answer should have an impact on the kind of mortgage you choose.
- **Habit 4: Think Win-Win** — Your mortgage transaction should benefit *both* of you, not just the mortgage lender.

You wouldn't necessarily marry the first person you date. How can you assure that you don't fall victim to the first loan officer you encounter?

First, let me assure you that although my title was senior loan officer, my primary role was that of *salesperson*.

Second, approach the meeting with the goal of sitting down with the loan officer and going through the process. Once.

You'll probably need to bring your latest W-2 forms and your tax forms from the last couple of years with you. Then you'll work on completing a standardized form with the loan officer, known as the Uniform Residential Loan Application. This form is also known by its Fannie Mae and Freddie Mac form number, 1003 or "ten-oh-three."

On the 1003 you will indicate things like:

- o   Your address
- o   Place of employment
- o   Family information
- o   Earnings
- o   Assets
- o   Liabilities

Allow at least an hour for this process. In the meantime, don't be surprised if the loan officer attempts to *bond* with you. (And I had loan applicants, especially the ones who came in for 7:30 P.M. appointments it seemed, drag this interview process on for hours as I learned much more from them than I ever needed or *wanted* to know.)

Get all of your questions answered during this process. Become an educated consumer. *But don't make any decisions yet.* (Just as you might reserve judgment if your first date asked you, "Will you marry me?")

At the conclusion of your meeting, your loan officer should provide you with two completed standardized documents:

1. **Good Faith Estimate (GFE) — See Exhibit 1** — This form is similar to the Manufacturer's Suggested Retail Price sticker you will see slapped on the window of a new car. The GFE will provide you with a close approximation of the fees the mortgage lender will charge you. Hang on to this form and bring it to the closing meeting with you. Compare the fees you were charged with the fees the lender said you would be charged. If the amounts significantly differ, demand an explanation. If you are not satisfied, be prepared to walk out of the closing.

2. **Truth-In-Lending (TIL) Statement — See Exhibit 2** — This sheet will detail the actual costs over the life of the loan.

Exhibit 1

GOOD FAITH ESTIMATE
(Not a Loan Commitment)

Lender:	Sales Price: 152800.00
Address:	Base Loan Amount: 148216.00
Applicant(s):	Total Loan Amount: 151550.00
	Interest Rate: 8.2500
	Type of Loan: FHA
Property Address:	Preparation Date: 04/11/00
	Loan Number:

The information provided below reflects estimates of the charges which you are likely to incur at the settlement of your loan. The fees listed are estimates - actual charges may be more or less. Your transaction may not involve a fee for every item listed. The numbers listed beside the estimates generally correspond to the numbered lines contained in the HUD-1 or HUD-1A settlement statement which you will be receiving at settlement. The HUD-1 or HUD-1A settlement statement will show you the actual cost of items paid at settlement.

"A" designates those costs affecting APR.   "P" designates compensation to Broker not paid out of Loan Proceeds.

800	ITEMS PAYABLE IN CONNECTION WITH LOAN:			1000	RESERVES DEPOSITED WITH LENDER	
801 A	Origination Due Lender @ 1.0000	$ 1482.16		1001	Hazard Insurance Impounds	$ 25.00
802 A	Discount @	$		1002 A	Mortgage Insurance Impounds	
803	Appraisal Fee	$ *250.00		1004	Property Tax Impounds	$ 1050.00
804	Credit Report	$ *52.00		1006	Flood Insurance Impounds	$
805 A	Lender's Inspection Fee	$ 35.00		1007		$
808 A	Tax Service Contract	$ *52.00		1008		$
809 A	Underwriting Review	$		1009	Aggregate Analysis Adjustment	$
810 A	Administration Fee	$ 16.00		1100	TITLE CHARGES:	
811 A	Application Fee	$		1101	Settlement or Closing Fee	$
812 A	Commitment Fee	$		1105	Document Preparation Fee	$
813 A	Warehouse Fee / Interest Differential	$		1106	Notary Fee	$
814 P	Yield Sprd. Prem. ____ % $			1107	Attorney Fee	$
815 P	Serv. Rel. Prem. ____ % $			1108	Title Insurance Premium	$ 518.00
816 A	Origination Due Broker @	$		1111	Endorsement Fee	$ 75.00
817 A	FHA Upfront MIP / VA Funding Fee	$ 3334.86		1112	TITLE EXAM AND BINDER	$ 200.00
818 A	SETTLEMENT FEE	$ 225.00				
819 A	FLOOD CERT & COURIER FEE	26.50		1200	GOVERNMENT RECORDER AND TRANSFER CHARGES:	
820 A		$				
821 A		$		1201	Recording Fee	$ 60.00
822 A		$		1202	City/County tax / stamps	$
823 A		$		1203	State tax / stamps	$
824 A		$		1204		$
825 A		$				
900	ITEMS REQUIRED BY LENDER TO BE PAID IN ADVANCE:			1300	ADDITIONAL SETTLEMENT CHARGES:	
901 A	Prepaid Interest 15 days @ $ 34.25	$ 513.82		1301	Survey	$ 140.00
902 A	Mortgage Insurance Premium	$		1302	Termite Inspection	$ *95.00
903	Hazard Insurance Premium	$ 300.00		1303	Property Inspection	$
904	Flood Insurance Premium	$		1304	Photo Fee	$
				1305		$
				1306		$
				1307		$
				1308		$

TOTAL ESTIMATED MONTHLY PAYMENT		TOTAL ESTIMATED FUNDS NEEDED TO CLOSE	
Principal and Interest	$ 1138.55	Total Purchase Price / Existing Payoff	$152800.00
Real Estate Taxes	$ 175.00	Estimated Closing Costs	$ 6112.52
Hazard Insurance	$ 25.00	Estimated Prepaid Items / Reserves	$ 1888.82
Mortgage Insurance	$ 61.76	Total Paid Items & Subordinate Financing	$
Homeowners Association Dues	$	Seller Paid Closing Costs	$
Second Principal and Interest	$	FHA UFMIP/VA Funding Fee	$ 3334.00
Other	$	Base Loan Amount	$148216.00
TOTAL MONTHLY PAYMENT	$ 1400.31	TOTAL ESTIMATED FUNDS NEEDED TO CLOSE	$ 9251.33

These estimates are provided pursuant to the Real Estate Settlement Procedures Act of 1974, as amended (RESPA). Additional information can be found in the HUD Special Information Booklet, which is to be provided to you by your Mortgage Broker or lender if your application is to purchase residential real property and the lender will take a first lien on the property. The undersigned acknowledges receipt of a copy of the Special Information Booklet "Settlement Costs."

| Applicant _____ | Date 4/11/00 | Applicant _____ | Date 4-11-00 |

This Good Faith Estimate is being provided by

Page 1 of 2

GFELEND1 (05/97)   Printed by The Loan Handler from Contour Software, Inc. (408) 370-1700

Exhibit 2

FEDERAL TRUTH-IN-LENDING DISCLOSURE STATEMENT
(MADE IN COMPLIANCE WITH FEDERAL LAW)

Lender/Broker: ▓▓▓▓▓▓▓▓▓▓▓▓▓▓▓▓▓▓
Loan No.: ▓▓▓▓▓▓▓▓▓▓▓▓▓▓▓▓   Date: 04/11/00
Borrower(s): ▓▓▓▓▓▓▓▓▓▓▓▓

Property Address: ▓▓▓▓▓▓▓▓▓▓▓▓▓▓▓

[X] Initial Disclosure estimated at time of application   [ ] Final Disclosure based on contract terms

ANNUAL PERCENTAGE RATE The cost of your credit as a yearly rate.	FINANCE CHARGE The dollar amount the credit will cost you assuming the annual percentage rate does not change.	Amount Financed The amount of credit provided to you or on your behalf as of loan closing.	Total of Payments The amount you will have paid after you have made all payments as scheduled assuming the annual percentage rate does not change.
E 8.940 %	E $ 268864.48	E $ 145916.66	E $ 414781.14

YOUR PAYMENT SCHEDULE WILL BE:

NUMBER OF PAYMENTS	*AMOUNT OF PAYMENTS	WHEN PAYMENTS ARE DUE MONTHLY BEGINNING	NUMBER OF PAYMENTS	*AMOUNT OF PAYMENTS	WHEN PAYMENTS ARE DUE MONTHLY BEGINNING
12	1200.08	06/01/2000			
12	1199.57	06/01/2001			
12	1199.01	06/01/2002			
12	1198.40	06/01/2003			
12	1197.74	06/01/2004			
12	1197.02	06/01/2005			
10	1196.24	06/01/2006			
278	1138.55	04/01/2007			

* Includes mortgage insurance premiums, excludes taxes, hazard insurance or flood insurance.

[ ] **DEMAND FEATURE:** This loan transaction has a demand feature.

[ ] **VARIABLE RATE FEATURE:** Your loan contains a Variable Rate Feature. Disclosures about the Variable Rate Feature have been provided to you separately.

SECURITY INTEREST: You are giving a security interest in:
[X] the goods or property being purchased. [ ] real property you already own.
FILING OR RECORDING FEES $ 60.00
LATE CHARGE: If a payment is more than 15 days late, you will be charged $ 56.01 / 4 % of the total payment past due.

PREPAYMENT: If you pay off your loan early, you
[ ] may [X] will not have to pay a penalty.
[X] may [ ] will not be entitled to a refund of part of the finance charge.

INSURANCE: Credit life, accident, health or loss of income insurance is not required in connection with this loan. This loan transaction requires the following insurance:
[X] Hazard Insurance [ ] Flood Insurance [ ] Private Mortgage Insurance [X] Mutual Mortgage Insurance
Borrower(s) may obtain hazard and flood insurance through any person of his/her choice, provided said carrier meets the requirements of the Lender. If Borrower desires Property Insurance to be obtained through the Lender's designated agency, the cost will be set forth in a separate insurance statement furnished by the Lender.

ASSUMPTION: Someone buying your house
[ ] may [X] may, subject to conditions, [ ] may not assume the remainder of your loan on the original terms.

See your contract documents for additional information regarding nonpayment, default, right to accelerate the maturity of the obligation, prepayment rebates and penalties, and the Lender's policy regarding assumption of the obligation.

[X] all dates and numerical disclosures except late payment disclosures are estimates. E means an estimate.

The undersigned hereby acknowledge receiving and reading a completed copy of this disclosure along with copies of the documents provided. The delivery and signing of this disclosure does not constitute an obligation on the part of the lender to make, or the Borrower(s) to accept, the loan as identified.

Read, acknowledged and accepted this 11 day of APRIL 2010 By: ▓▓▓▓▓▓▓▓

▓▓▓▓▓▓▓ (Borrower)   ▓▓▓▓▓▓▓ (Borrower)

▓▓▓▓▓▓▓ (Borrower)   ▓▓▓▓▓▓▓ (Borrower)

Boxes are checked if applicable.

Chapter Fifteen

More About the Good Faith Estimate

The Good Faith Estimate would disclose such costs as:

- o Origination fee
- o Other closing costs
  - ➤ Application fee
  - ➤ Title search fee
  - ➤ Recording fee
  - ➤ Flood certification fee
  - ➤ Closing fee
- o Escrows for property taxes, hazard insurance, and interest

Most of the costs are for services required by law. In theory, the mortgage lender should simply pass along the fees from third-party providers without markup.

For instance, even though I live miles from the nearest significant body of water, my state requires a *flood certification* every time I refinance my mortgage.

I would be leery of what are called *junk fees*, such as a "document preparation fee." Why pay an additional $500 for what the mortgage company should be doing anyway as part of its job?

Look at the *total* of closing costs. That is what really matters. Although it may vary upon where you live, **a total of $1,500 to $2,500 in closing costs** would be considered reasonable.

As you can see from the above list, some of the costs that appear on the Good Faith Estimate are not fees at all but are monies put into *escrow* (a reserve). In that way, when your property tax bill or your home insurance bill comes due, there will be money set aside to pay them.

A side note: Under certain circumstances, you may elect to pay your property taxes directly rather than have them paid through escrow, but you may be assessed a fee to do so. The lender may be required to pay for the services of a "big brother" — an agency that will monitor you to ensure taxes are indeed paid!

Chapter Sixteen

Will You Need to Pay a Service Release
Premium
or a Pre-payment Penalty?

O ne of the most important indicators on the Truth-In-Lending Statement is whether or not you will need to pay a penalty if you pay back your loan early. If you pay off a high-interest mortgage early, the secondary lender will not be too happy about it. After all, he may have already slipped a hefty Service Release Premium (the "kickback") to the primary lender and will lose a stream of gigantic interest payments from you in the future. So, to partially compensate him, he may require a pre-payment penalty from you. If so, it will be indicated on the Truth-In-Lending Statement. Be sure to notice if the appropriate box is checked (or left un-checked).

NOTE: Just being sure that your mortgage does not con-tain a Service Release Premium or a pre-payment penalty could save you several thousand dollars. Notice now— before it's too late.

Chapter Seventeen

Let's Go Mortgage Shopping

STEP 1

After you are armed with a typical and completed Good Faith Estimate and Truth-In-Lending Statement, you are ready to do your comparison shopping.

Do not fall for the overtures of your first loan officer. If he or she is unethical, he or she may try to steer you into the highest-rate mortgage program available just to see if you will bite; while in reality, you could qualify for a much more favorable interest rate. The difference between a thirty-year fixed rate mortgage at six percent and the same mortgage at eight percent is more than $72,000 in additional interest over the life of the loan. So by falling for this trick of your first loan officer up-selling you the rate, you could spend *thousands* of extra dollars.

Instead, contact a half dozen other potential suitors for your mortgage (these could include traditional banks, mortgage banks and mortgage brokers) either by phone, e-mail, U.S. mail, or by fax. Say:

"I'm interested in obtaining a mortgage. My credit score is (you would know the number after meeting with your first loan officer). Would you please fax me a Good Faith Estimate and a Truth-In-Lending Statement to my fax machine at 555-1212?"

The person on the other end of the line will know that they are dealing with a professional. They will know they will *not* be doing business with a good old boy who has spaghetti-stained W-2 forms in his back pocket.

And it sounds a lot better than calling to ask, "Duh, what is your rate?"

STEP 2

When you contact the other potential sources of your funds, indicate the following:

o   The amount you wish to finance
o   The types of mortgages you are interested in
o   The value of your property
o   Your credit score
o   How you wish to receive a reply (by return fax, e-mail or regular mail)

Some of the lenders you contact may not respond. (They'd rather spend their time trying to hoodwink good old boys and girls!) Some of the lenders may have fees that are astronomical. You can quickly eliminate them. Concentrate on the three or four that look promising.

The ball is now in your court.

SHOULD YOU DO BUSINESS WITH A MORTGAGE COMPANY OVER THE INTERNET?

It never hurts to get more information on this process, if you can do it quickly and efficiently. One of the most comprehensive personal financial Web sites I have found is www.bankrate.com. Invariably you will run into a snag somewhere during the processing of your mortgage. It can be helpful to have a real, live and local person to turn to. But you might be able to use an online quote to negotiate an even better "in-person" deal. In that way you can have the best of both worlds.

Chapter Eighteen

A Word About
Your Credit Report

Your credit report has a major bearing on what kind of mortgage you can get.

Some things to keep in mind:

- o How you have paid your mortgage (if you have had one) is shown near the top of your report. "The past is the best predictor of the future" is the mantra of your potential mortgage lender. As a result, whatever you do, *always* pay your mortgage on time. (I have my mortgage payment directly withdrawn from my checking account. That way, if the payment is late, it is the mortgage company's fault, not mine.)
- o Your all-important credit score. Credit scores are a relatively new factor in mortgage lending.

Why do you think credit scores were created? The most common credit score was developed in 1989 by the Fair Isaac Corporation (and is known as the *FICO score*) so that an objective, mathematical formula could be applied to all loan applicants. No lender wants to be accused of discriminatory lending practices.

As a loan officer I'd often be asked, "How many points can I add to my credit score if I pay off a credit card or satisfy a collection item?"

The formula for calculating credit scores is proprietary. That means that the people who calculate it won't release how they do it. And they also occasionally change their own formula.

The credit score does *not* consider the following:
- o Occupation
- o Employer
- o Employment history
- o Income
- o Assets

The credit score *does* consider these factors:
- o Payment history
- o Outstanding credit
- o Credit history
- o Type of credit
- o Public records

Let's look at these one at a time.

Payment history
- o Have you been late on any bills?
- o If so, how recently?
- o What is the proportion of late payments to on-time payments?
- o *Not as harmful to miss payments on accounts with low balances rather than high ones because lenders stand to lose less money on low balances.*

Outstanding credit
- o Are you close to or beyond your credit limit?

o How much credit is available to you, even if your balances are currently low?

o *You may never be too rich or have too many friends, but having the temptation of too much credit available can negatively affect your credit score.*

Credit history

o How long have you had your various accounts?

o *Fewer than five credit lines in the last two years is considered a short history.*

o How many new accounts have you opened recently?

o How many inquiries (requests for credit) have you made in the last year?

Type of credit

o Are your accounts installment loans, bankcards, department store cards or mortgages?

o *In general, diversity is a positive factor.*

Public records

o Court judgments such as liens or bankruptcies are strong negatives, as are accounts turned over to collection agencies.

The credit scoring formula will change to reflect current lending patterns.

Your credit score will change whenever information on your credit report is updated.

Your score will range from 375 to 900. A score of 650 or higher is considered *very good* by most mortgage lenders, 700 or higher is *excellent*.

In my experience in the industry, I never saw a score either below 500 or above 800.

Negative information can remain on your file for up to seven years from the date it first appears. Bankruptcies can appear for up to ten years.

Credit inquiries (inquiries regarding your credit status when you apply for a bank loan, mortgage, or charge card) can appear for up to two years.

Q: Are credit inquiries good or bad?
A: They can negatively impact your credit score.

Q: Why? I'm just shopping around, trying to get the best rate or deal.
A: People anticipating a financial downturn try to increase the amount of credit they have available. That's why too many recent credit inquires on your record can be a bad thing.

According to the National Association for Financial Education, one in four credit reports contains errors.

If you have a common name or a relative has a similar name, be especially careful. Even though you and the other party obviously have different social security numbers, don't be surprised if some of their information shows up on *your* credit report. (I wonder if NASCAR drivers Dale Earnhart and Dale Earnhart, Jr. ever had such issues.)

When a couple marries they also join their credit histories (for better or for worse).

A word of warning: If you find that you or your spouse can not resist the constant barrage of credit card offers you receive in the mail and you get in debt over your head, you may want to contact an agency that counsels consumers on credit. The agency may be able to lower your payments or your interest rates or even eliminate some of your debt altogether. But it may come at a price.

I had more than one potential borrower tell me, "I never realized the impact the actions of the agency would have on my credit report. For me, it was a worse black mark on my record than a bankruptcy."

SIGN ON A PHONE POLE: "CALL NOW TO GET YOUR CREDIT FIXED INSTANTLY"

If you're trying to fix a problematic credit report, don't waste your money on "credit-repair" firms, which often over-promise and charge big fees for things you can do yourself.

Check out the Federal Trade Commission Web site for helpful credit-repair advice: www.ftc.gov.

THREE CREDIT REPORTING AGENCIES

The three credit reporting agencies are:
- o Equifax (www.equifax.com)
- o Experian (www.experian.com)
- o TransUnion (www.transunion.com)

Note: Your information will not necessarily be the same on all three credit reports.

So why are there three different credit reporting agencies? Wouldn't it be easier if there were just *one* agency to deal with?

For the answer, take a look at the market for college entrance exams. High school juniors and seniors have the option of taking either or both of the ACT and the SAT exams. Why? My guess is that the second service saw how profitable it was to provide testing for college. (After all, how many millions of high school students apply to colleges each year?) So the second service decided to enter the fray. And there can be enough business for the two (or three) players.

50

Chapter Nineteen

Identity Theft

C all 877-322-8228 or go to www.annualcreditreport.com and get your free credit report from each of the three credit reporting agencies. Here's why:

After I finished writing the previous chapter of this book, I was standing in the office supply section of my local store considering the purchase of a shredder. An elderly couple turned to me and said, "We recently had our apartment broken into. The thief took our records with him. We became victims of identity theft. We don't want this to happen again. What kind of shredder would you recommend?"

Since we just spoke about credit reports, let's take a moment (with the help of the United States Postal Inspection Service) to take a look at their concerns.

Identity theft is America's fastest growing crime. It occurs when a crook steals key pieces of personal identifying information such as a name, address, date of birth, Social Security number, and mother's maiden name to gain access to a person's financial accounts. Armed with this information, an identity thief may open new credit or financial accounts, buy cars, apply for loans or Social Security benefits, rent an apartment, or set up utility and phone service in someone else's name.

What you can do to protect your identity:

Deposit outgoing mail at a Post Office, in a blue U.S. Postal Service collection box, or give it directly to your letter carrier.

Shred unwanted documents that contain personal information before discarding them, using a *crosscut* shredder. (A crosscut shredder destroys documents more thoroughly.)

Review your consumer credit reports annually.

Check whether the major credit reporting agencies have accounts in your name that were opened without your consent. Ask them to place a "fraud alert" on your line.

Report credit card fraud to one of the major credit reporting agencies, either online or by phone. (Due to a recent change designed to help consumers, you can report the incident to any of the three agencies, as they now share a common database.)

Equifax: 800-525-6285 www.equifax.com

Experian: 888-397-3742 www.experian.com

TransUnion: 800-680-7289 www.transunion.com

Never give personal information over the phone or the Internet unless you initiated the contact.

- Sign your new credit cards—before someone else does.
- Memorize your Social Security number and passwords; don't carry them with you. Don't use your date of birth as your password.
- Don't ever leave receipts behind—at ATMs, on counters at financial institutions or at gasoline pumps.
- Check expiration dates on credit cards and contact the issuer if you don't get a replacement before they expire. Ditto for monthly financial statements and bills.
- Report ID theft online with the Federal Trade Commission at www.consumer.gov/idtheft, or call its Identity Theft Hotline at 1-877-IDTHEFT.

How to keep personal information safe from online prowlers:

Never input your credit card or other financial account numbers at a Web site unless it offers a secure transaction. A secure (or "encrypted") transaction will have an icon of a lock in the bottom strip of the Web browser page and the URL address for the Web page will change from "http" to "https" for the page on which you input the personal data.
Should you need to contact the credit card companies, here are their Web sites:

American Express: www10.americanexpress.com
Discover: www.discovercard.com/discover/data/products
MasterCard: www.mastercard.com.

Identity theft is the fastest growing crime in America. Learn to protect yourself.

Chapter Twenty

What is the Difference Between "Loan Pre-qualification" and "Loan Pre-approval"?

One Sunday my wife and I were out looking at houses (as many couples like to do).

One house was particularly striking. It had a walk-in *cedar-lined* closet in the master bedroom.

So I asked the Realtor, "How much?"

She replied, "440" (as in four hundred and forty thousand dollars).

Gulp!

Now, if she had only known our financial condition at the time, she would have either charged us to come in the door and waste her time or not let us in at all.

Most house shoppers were like us—go find something you like then see if, or how, you can afford it.

When you put your house on the market, you will find a lot of couples like we were. Clueless.

That is why, as an astute buyer, it pays to do things differently. Before you go looking for a house, become *pre-approved* with a lender.

In essence this means you are ready to go with a mortgage. You just need to fill in the lines that have the amount of the loan and the address of the property.

The seller and the Realtor will be so happy to see you. They have tired from dealing with couples like we were. When you are *pre-approved*, you will have real negotiating power. You stand out from the crowd. You *will* be taken seriously.

A pre-approval:

- o A thorough verification of financial facts
- o You will receive a pre-approval letter that you can show to the seller and Realtor
- o "Next best thing to a line of credit"
- o Can give you leverage in purchase negotiations

A *pre-qualification*, on the other hand, is simply a cursory review of your finances.

A loan officer may have looked at your credit score, your earnings, and your level of debt and announced, "Looks like you could afford a $200,000 house."

At least that used to be the distinction between a loan pre-approval and a loan pre-qualification.

Now, according to Valerie Patterson, senior producer of *The Wall Street Journal's* online real estate section, www.realestatejournal.com, the increased number of lenders with varying standards (or even lack of standards) has diluted the effect of the loan pre-approval letter.

According to a survey by Campbell Communications for the trade publication Inside Mortgage News of more than 1,700 real estate agents and brokers concerning their relationships and attitudes toward mortgage providers, a majority of the agents and brokers reported that faulty pre-approval letters were the top complaint with lenders.

In fact, many of them didn't believe the letters were worth the paper they had been written on.

Chapter Twenty-one

Should You Rent or Buy?

An apartment management company was losing their tenants. Apparently, many of these tenants were infatuated with the idea of owning their own home. They were lured by unbelievable, cut-rate deals advertised by local builders in the Sunday newspaper. And they were leaving in droves.

The tenants were simply thinking, "Let's stop throwing our money down the drain on rent — let's buy a house."

I was asked to speak to their apartment rental agents to address the issue. I told them:

"According to *The Wall Street Journal*, contrary to popular opinion, renting can often be the better alternative, especially if there's a chance you'll stay put less than five years."

Making the choice of home ownership, like making the choice to marry or to have children requires careful consideration.

Generally, homeownership is a good idea. But let's take a look at the facts:

In the initial years of your mortgage, *ninety percent or more* of your monthly payment will be going toward interest expense.

Over the life of a thirty-year mortgage on $150,000 at six percent, you will pay $173,757 in interest expense. This is real money and, as you can see, is more than the original price of the home.

On a thirty-year mortgage, it won't be until *year nineteen* that *half* of your monthly payment will be applied toward the principal. Until then, *most* of your monthly payment will still be spent on interest expense. As a homeowner, you will also be making payments for:

- Property taxes
- Homeowner's insurance
- Utilities
- Maintenance
- Decorating
- Landscaping

while possibly giving up amenities like swimming pools and other common areas.

Interest-only loans can be a great way to *initially* keep down your monthly payment. But you'll only be paying more interest later on a *higher balance*.

What if property values go *down*? According to PMI Mortgage Insurance Company, the following metropolitan areas face the biggest pricing correction:
- Los Angeles–Long Beach, CA
- Sacramento–Arden, CA
- Riverside–San Bernardino, CA
- Edison, NJ

And according to the PMI U.S. Market Risk Index report, these cities are also likely candidates for a downturn in housing prices:

- Boston, MA
- San Diego, CA
- Long Island, NY
- Santa Ana, CA
- Oakland, CA

Nationwide, there is a 21.8 percent chance that overall house prices across the 50 largest housing markets will see prices fall.

Most of us have had the experience of owning a *car* that is worth less than what we owed on it. This is called being "upside down" or "under water" with respect to the auto loan. Similarly, you could have negative equity in your home, maybe trapping you in place *for years*. What if then you had to move suddenly? You would lose a lot more than just the few hundred dollars tied up in a month's rent and a security deposit as you might if you were still in your apartment. Instead, you could lose thousands.

As unpleasant as it might be, be sure to read and understand *all* of the fine print of the mortgage. For example, is the mortgage you are being offered an **ARM** (adjustable rate mortgage)? If so, *how often* can the rate be adjusted and by how much? Is this just a "teaser," below-market, short-term rate to get you into the property, with you possibly suffering the consequences of a much higher rate later?

Chapter
Twenty-two

If You Buy, Don't Buy a Starter House

G ary, the best man at my wedding, bought a house. It was a fine house—for a bachelor. After he started dating Pat and they decided to get married, Pat declared, "This house will never do for the both of us." So Gary sold *his* house to buy *their* home.

Avoid buying the starter house. It may seem large now in comparison to your tiny apartment, but you'll only be in the house a year or two before deciding to have children or deciding the house is otherwise too small. Instead, continue to save your money for a down payment on a larger house that you could comfortably live in for a half dozen or more years. Why go through the process of closing twice, moving twice, and all of the associated fees in such a short period of time?

Further, if you decide to move, you may pay a Realtor a commission to sell your home. At six percent, the fee would be $9,000 on a $150,000 home. The closing costs on a new mortgage could be another $1,500 to $2,500. Again, this is real money. You could have over $10,000 in move-related expenses, and the moving van hasn't even pulled up to your door yet.

Moral: Since the impact can cost you thousands of dollars, be sure to make decisions involving the selling of any house and moving both carefully and wisely.

Chapter
Twenty-three

What Kind of Mortgage
Should I Get?

Walking into a mortgage company these days is like walking into a homemade ice cream shop in one substantial way: the flavors seem to change every day. Furthermore, the flavors seem to change as you go from company to company, making it sometimes difficult to make a valid "taste" comparison.

Let's discuss the three basic "flavors":

VANILLA

The basic mortgage has a *fixed* rate. This rate is determined at some point between the time of the application for the loan and the time of closing. Like the price of stocks, the rate will fluctuate every day, but most loan officers will attempt to "upsell" the rate (at least a little bit) before quoting the rate to you in an attempt to earn additional commission. The rate will then be in effect for the entire life of the loan, usually fifteen or thirty years.

CHOCOLATE

This mortgage has a *variable* rate. This kind of mortgage is called an ARM (for Adjustable Rate Mortgage).

Because of the risk involved (to you), the variable rate will generally be less than the prevailing fixed rate.

If you choose an ARM, know the following:
- o How often the rate can change
- o By how much the rate can change
- o What is the maximum rate you can be charged.

TWIST

This mortgage will have characteristics of both of the above. For example, I sold my in-laws (and I really *do* like them) a 7/23 ARM.

This meant that their rate was fixed for the first seven years and then it would be adjustable for each of the next twenty-three years.

This option made sense to them because they lived in a small starter home and knew that they would be moving to a bigger house within the first half-dozen years.

The benefit: they got a rate that was less than the current thirty-year fixed mortgage rate.

The downside: if they stayed in the house longer than they had planned, they might need to re-finance their loan.

OTHER FLAVORS

Those are the three basic "flavors" of mortgages. But you might find, after talking with your loan officer, that the best flavor for you is "mango tangerine tutti-frutti." For instance, you may elect to secure a mortgage with a different loan-to-value percentage. *Loan-to-value* (LTV) relates the amount of the loan to the appraised value of the property. Eighty percent, ninety percent, or, in a higher risk case, even 110 percent are typical LTVs. Homeowners who are refinancing—especially to consolidate or pay off other high-interest debts, may seek a higher LTV in their mortgages. With higher LTVs come higher interest rates.

SHOULD I GET A 30-YEAR OR A 15-YEAR MORTGAGE?

Before we answer the question, let's look at the facts.

Let's assume you were looking at these two options on a $100,000 loan at seven percent. Typically, the rate on a fifteen-year mortgage will be less than the rate on a thirty-year mortgage—maybe a quarter-point difference—because there is less risk to the lender over a shorter period of time. But let's keep it simple in our example and assume the same rate in either case. The figures would look like this:

	15 year	30 year
Monthly payment	$899	$665
Total money spent	$161,789	$239,509
Total interest paid	$61,789	$139,509

Your payment on a thirty-year mortgage would be $234 less each month but you would end up paying an additional $77,720 in interest over time.

Does this mean you should *always* opt for the lesser-term mortgage to avoid the additional charges?

Not necessarily.

One of the keys to life in general is to live with intentionality. This means to always know why you are doing what you are doing.

Before my wife and I bought our first house, another young couple down the street bought their first home and opted for a fifteen-year mortgage. Here's why.

They had a newborn son they wanted to eventually send to a private high school. By selecting a fifteen-year mortgage, they would have their house paid for by the time their child entered ninth grade. The resulting cash flow would allow them to attain their goal.

Pretty smart thinking! (I wish my wife and I had had similar foresight at that age.)

For them, a fifteen-year mortgage made sense, but for you it may not.

A possible option: Elect the thirty-year mortgage, then make additional payments when you are able. Be sure that the extra monies are applied directly to the *principal* (and not toward principal *and* interest).

I'VE HEARD I CAN SAVE THOUSANDS OF DOLLARS BY MAKING MY MORTGAGE PAYMENTS TWICE A MONTH RATHER THAN ONCE A MONTH. HOW DOES THAT WORK?

Well, it's not exactly twice a month.

Rather than making twelve monthly payments, you send your money in every two weeks. As a result, you'll make twenty-six bi-weekly payments a year.

This is like making an additional *monthly* payment each year.

Here's the savings you could claim on a $100,000, thirty-year loan at a seven and one-half percent interest rate:

	Monthly	**Bi-weekly**
Payment	$699	$350
Total interest paid	$151,717	$113,478
Length of payments	30 years	23 years

Your savings in interest would be $38,239 while paying off your loan approximately seven years earlier.

But you may ask, "How can a couple of extra payments make such a big difference?"

We indicated before that in the early years ninety percent or more of your mortgage payment would be directed toward interest rather than principal.

To keep our example simple, let's assume your monthly mortgage payment is $1,000; so, less than $100 of that payment would go toward the principal.

If you were to make just one additional monthly payment (or two bi-weekly payments) per year, you would be paying the equivalent of more than ten months of your regular principal payments.

With a lower principal balance, more of your subsequent payments can then be directed toward the principal rather than toward interest.

Moral: An additional principal-only payment each year can get the snowball rolling downhill quickly!

WARNING: You may receive solicitations in the mail from vendors quoting these kinds of savings for bi-weekly mortgage programs. Then they'll ask you for a fee (sometimes in the hundreds of dollars) to set up a program for you. You can usually do this yourself, at **NO COST**. Just be sure that all additional payments are directed solely to your mortgage principal.

DOESN'T THE EXISTING MORTGAGE RATE DEPEND ON THE PRIME RATE?

You just heard that the Fed has reduced the prime rate. (The *prime rate* is the interest rate charged by banks to their most creditworthy customers.) Great! Won't this have a positive effect on mortgage rates?

Only indirectly. The prime rate has a bigger effect on *short-term financing*, such as auto loans.

The mortgage rate, being a long-term loan, is tied to longer-term financial instruments, such as the yield on the ten- or thirty-year Treasury bond.

RATE ENVY

Borrowers (especially *male* borrowers) like to brag to their neighbors over the fence about the low mortgage rate they were able to secure on a refinance.

I was no different.

A few years ago I went to refinance my eight and five-eighths percent mortgage to a lower rate (not at my mortgage company but at a bank).

At the time of application, they were offering a rate of 6.99 percent. But being the astute mortgage professional I am, I had kept up on my financial reading. Everything I had read indicated that rates were headed downward.

"Would you like to lock the rate?" the loan officer asked me. This means that the bank would guarantee the rate when it came time to close the loan.

Mortgage rates, like stock prices, fluctuate each day. This is why I always find it humorous to find some mortgage companies advertising rates in the newspaper.

You figure that if you see a mortgage rate quoted in the Sunday newspaper, it was probably the rate for Thursday and now the caller can ask for the same rate the following Monday. Can you imagine calling your stockbroker on Monday and asking to buy or sell a stock at last Thursday's closing price?

Anyway, I announced proudly and confidently to the loan officer, "No, I won't lock the rate, I'll float." *Float* means that I would lock in the rate at a later date.

Two weeks later I received a call from the bank. "Mr. Janusz, we are ready to close your loan."

"What do you mean?" I stammered. My mortgage company would have taken at least twice as long to process the loan. I thought I had plenty of time, so I hadn't been following the market.

"What is today's rate?" I asked.

"Seven and one-quarter percent."

"Darn!" Not only had rates not gone down, they had actually gone *up*. So much for the advice of experts!

"Do you want to lock now, or wait until tomorrow to lock? If so, tomorrow will be your last chance."

I was greedy. I wanted to at least get that quarter-point back and reduce the rate down to seven percent.

"I'll float," I replied.

Guess what the rate was the *next* day? Seven and three-eighths percent!

Moral of the story: find a rate that you can live with. Lock it in. Get on with your life.

On a $100,000 loan with a term of thirty years, the difference of a one-quarter percentage point can mean a savings of more than $17 a month or more than $6,000 over the life of the loan. But the average American moves once every seven years. And you may refinance long before that.

Chapter
Twenty-four

The Financing Odd Couple:
Fannie Mae and Freddie Mac

You won't be in the mortgage maze for very long before you hear the name of the two patron saints of mortgage lending, Fannie Mae and Freddie Mac. Who are they?

In 1938, the federal government established *Fannie Mae* to expand the flow of mortgage money by creating a secondary market. In 1968, Fannie Mae became a private company operating with private capital on a self-sustaining basis. Its role was expanded to buy mortgages beyond traditional government loan limits. Today, Fannie Mae operates under a congressional charter that directs it to channel efforts to increase the availability and affordability of homeownership for low- to moderate- and middle-income Americans.

Similarly, *Freddie Mac* is a stockholder-owned corporation chartered by Congress in 1970 to keep money flowing to mortgage lenders in support of homeownership and rental housing.

You and I are not able to get mortgage funds directly from either Fannie Mae or Freddie Mac since they are *secon-*

dary lenders. However, they generally offer the best terms on mortgage lending to *primary* lenders such as banks and even my former mortgage company. But, to get these good rates through a primary lender, you must meet Fannie Mae's and Freddie Mac's terms, which should be consistent no matter where you apply for a mortgage.

If you are unable to meet these requirements, then you may need to settle for more expensive rates and terms from what are known as *sub-prime* or non-conforming lenders.

Chapter
Twenty-five

What is a "Debt-to-Income" Ratio?
Why is it so Important?

S econdary lenders such as Fannie Mae and Freddie Mac want to protect themselves. As a result, they want to be sure that, as a borrower of theirs, your mortgage obligation will not exceed a maximum amount of your income.

Specifically, they want no more than twenty-eight percent of your gross income to go toward housing. The total includes payments on the loan principal and interest, private mortgage insurance, hazard insurance, property taxes, and homeowner's association dues.

And they want no more than thirty-six percent of your income to go toward your total debts. This number refers to the maximum percentage of your monthly gross income that the lender allows for housing expenses plus recurring debt.

Recurring debt includes credit card payments, child support, car loans, and other obligations that will not be paid off within a relatively short period of time (six to ten months).

In reality, the "front-end" ratio of twenty-eight percent is the easier of the two to meet.

Here is why: Let's assume that your combined gross household income is $60,000 a year or $5,000 a month. (*Gross* is the larger figure, *net* is the smaller, after tax amount.) Twenty-eight percent of that amount means that you would be allowed to spend up to $1,400 on monthly housing expenses.

It is usually the "back-end" ratio of thirty-six percent that bites most people looking for a house. In this case the $1,800 maximum has to also include items like:

      o   One or more car payments (loan or lease)
      o   Credit card payments
      o   Student loans

Both you and your spouse have just bought new cars. So if you each have a $300 car payment, each of you has $100 in credit card payments and each of you is paying $50 in student loans, that only leaves a maximum of $900 in allowable housing expenses.

Moral: Buy the house first!

Chapter
Twenty-six

What is FHA?

C ongress knew they had to do something. And fast. The year was 1934. At the time, our country had two million unemployed construction workers. The government was concerned about a revolt among such a large constituency.

Congress acted. They created the Federal Housing Administration (FHA). Much like they would do for the Chrysler Corporation four decades later, the government would insure lenders against homebuyer default.

The programs they created would require low down payments and offer liberal underwriting guidelines. Rates would be offered that were one-half percent to one percent less than conventional rates.

About a half-million families become first-time homebuyers each year using FHA-insured loans.

Sounds great. So what's the catch?

What happens whenever the government gets involved? (Think: tax audit.) More red tape. More inspections. (Is there any lead-based paint in the house?)

Home sellers tend to shy away from buyers who are applying for FHA loans. At the very least, they know the loan approval process is liable to take a whole lot longer.

Chapter
Twenty-seven

What is VA?

This has nothing to do with the Commonwealth of Virginia, but is instead another government program. The Department of Veteran Affairs set up this form of assistance that resulted from the 1944 Serviceman's Readjustment Act (GI Bill of Rights).

The VA program requires no down payment and does not limit the size of the mortgage. Like FHA, it insures the lender against homebuyer default and typically offers below-market interest rates. If you are a veteran, you can get more information about the program at: www.homeloans.va.gov. Both veterans and non-veterans are eligible to buy foreclosed VA properties.

We loan officers avoided both FHA and VA programs—like the plague. Both limited the amount of fees we could charge the borrower and both were a whole lot more work than other mortgages.

More work. Less fees. Say, has anyone seen another Mr. LTP in the lobby?

Chapter Twenty-eight

Why do I Need an Appraisal?

O btaining an appraisal is one of the costliest items in the mortgage approval process. So why is it needed? The appraisal helps to determine the current market value of your property. In this way, the lender knows there is sufficient value backing up their investment in your property.

Q: I have an appraisal from a year ago. Is that good enough?

A: Probably not. The lender is interested in the *current* market value of your property. (Chances are, if your appraisal is from a year ago or longer, the value has even increased.)

The process goes like this: After getting information about your house, the appraiser attempts to locate and research two other properties that have sold in your neighborhood — one of a bit more value, another a bit less in value — and compares your property to each.

But don't bother to run the sweeper or pick up the kids' toys. Unlike a potential buyer who might be looking for *emo-*

emotional reasons, such as the color of the bedrooms of your house, the appraiser is looking at more objective criteria such as:

- o Number of square feet
- o Finished basement?
- o Deck?
- o Number of baths
- o Method of exterior construction

The appraiser will then compare the qualities of your house against others in your neighborhood that have sold most recently. He will make adjustments to come up with the approximate market value.

For instance, maybe the house down the street that just sold didn't have a deck. Yours does. The other house has a finished basement. Yours doesn't. The appraiser would adjust the figure on your house accordingly.

THE PRESSURE ON THE APPRAISERS

The appraiser is supposed to be an independent, objective third party in the transaction. His or her job is to do the research and, using their professional knowledge and experience, determine the market value of your home.

But, it is still a subjective opinion.

It would usually be in the best interest of both the borrower and the primary lender to have the market value be as high as possible. The primary lender will generally earn more commission if the mortgage is for a higher amount. The borrower will be able to get more money, especially for a "cash out" transaction. *Cash out* will allow the borrower to get money back at closing, maybe to pay off high-interest credit card debt or even to take a vacation.

We were one of the largest sources of mortgage origina-
tions in the city. Our company would fax dozens of requests
for appraisals each week.

First, we would know which appraisers were more (as we
called them) *aggressive* than others.

One particular appraiser we liked to use was *so aggressive*
in his assessment of property values that he was actually
blacklisted by a number of secondary lenders! They would
distrust and immediately throw out any of the inflated fig-
ures he would submit to them. We were counting on the fact
that other sources of wholesale funds did not yet know of
this appraiser's unsavory reputation.

If we knew that we needed a "stretch" appraisal to make
the deal work, we always knew what to do. "Get [Mr. Black-
listed]."

We designed a form that we would use to request any
appraisal. On the form we had a blank line on which we
would enter the *suggested* home market value before fax-
ing the form to the appraiser.

To better understand the situation, picture this: The typical appraisal business would be a "mom-and-pop"
operation. "Mom" would usually answer the phone and take
messages, while "pop" would be out in the field, taking digi-
tal pictures of houses or researching courthouse records.

For one of my favorite appraisal businesses, ninety percent of their business depended upon the orders we would
fax over to them. Look at it this way: Ninety percent of their
ability to put food on their table and a roof over their heads
depended on keeping us — the mortgage company — happy.

If you were running *their* business and a faxed order came
over the wire to you asking you to do your best to see
$250,000 worth of value in a property, wouldn't you try to
see it the mortgage company's way? Wouldn't you?

You may ask, "So what if the appraiser fudges a little on the value of my home? How will that hurt anything?"

According to a recent *Wall Street Journal* investigative article, it is this kind of pressure on appraisers that is partially to blame for the recent, sometimes artificial, rise in home prices.

Chapter
Twenty-nine

*Are Condominiums Treated Differently
Than Single-Family Houses?*

I n a word, yes. And here is why: With a condominium, you actually own only your *interior* space. You are thus dependent on the financial health and the moral responsibility of the developer or homeowners' association to maintain the exterior of your dwelling and to preserve your investment value over time. Will the developer still be interested in maintaining your property when you are ready to sell? Or will he have gone on to develop newer subdivisions?

Generally, freestanding condo units retain their value better than condos that are contained within a floor of a larger building.

If you purchase a condominium, be sure that it meets all Fannie Mae and Freddie Mac standards, such as the number of units per building, the amount of space between buildings and the number of developer-owned units. (Fannie Mae and Freddie Mac are the source of most conforming, lower-interest-rate mortgage loans.) If not, you may find it difficult to resell and you may force the next buyer into a non-conforming or sub-prime mortgage with a high interest rate.

To offset these additional costs to the buyer, you may then need to lower the price of the condominium, resulting in less profit for you.

Recently a condo developer in town fell into financial straits (maybe from offering too many "unbelievable" deals). Let's say at the same time you received a job offer for your dream job, but it would require you to relocate to Phoenix.

You have the "cream puff" unit of the neighborhood. The appraiser estimated its market value at $150,000. You'd be able to take the proceeds from your sale and make a nice down payment on a luxurious ranch in the desert. You can already see yourself basking in the February sun!

But the developer has to raise money quickly, so he's unloading his competing, twenty-four developer-owned units at fire-sale prices—at fifty cents on the dollar. How likely are you to get anything even close to the market value you are expecting?

A quick note: With any transaction involving property (and the investment of hundreds of thousands of dollars) it may be worthwhile to retain the services of a real-estate attorney (as a source of *unbiased* information). Better to be safe than sorry later.

Chapter Thirty

My Builder is Offering a Mortgage Interest Rate Below Any Other That I Have Been Quoted

O bviously, your builder is not a bank, but he *can* build the cost of financing back into the price of the house. To see if you are being offered a good deal, ask the builder for a price quote on your house if you were to obtain your own financing.

Before I moved into my current house, I asked the builder this question. I was able to save thousands on the purchase price of my house by getting a mortgage through a mortgage broker my Realtor had suggested.

On the other hand, before my fellow senior loan officer friend (the one who explained to me the motives behind the actions of the closing agent Ms. Dee Cupps) moved into his current house, he did the same thing. He found that the overall package offered by the builder was better than the financing he could get elsewhere, even considering he was financing a higher sales price for the home.

Chapter Thirty-one

FAQs (Five Frequently Asked Questions)

MY NEIGHBOR QUALIFIED FOR A SEVEN PERCENT MORTGAGE, THE BEST I CAN GET IS NINE PERCENT. WHY?

The mortgage interest rate depends on a lot of factors including:

      o Credit history

      o Employment

      o Type of property

Your neighbor may have a *prime* rate mortgage from Fannie Mae or Freddie Mac. You may need to settle for a *sub-prime* mortgage from a more expensive, private lender.

Fannie Mae and Freddie Mac do not buy "non-conforming" loans from lenders on the secondary market. In other words, you must be able to meet Fannie Mae's and Freddie Mac's terms and conditions to qualify for their loans.

WHY ARE SUB-PRIME MORTGAGES SUBJECT TO ABUSES?

We discussed a typical example of a sub-prime mortgage abuse when we examined the case of "Mr. LTP," the borrower with the spaghetti-stained W-2 forms.

There are two main reasons why sub-prime mortgages are ripe for abuses:

1. The lender knows that in many cases the borrower is desperate and knows about his past sins and knows he has few options. As a result, an unscrupulous lender could take advantage of the borrower with outrageous rates and closing costs.

2. In many cases the *Service Release Premium* (the "back-end fee" or "kickback" the primary lender receives from the secondary lender for closing the loan at a higher than necessary interest rate) does not even need to be disclosed on the closing Settlement Statement. And even when the Service Release Premium does appear on the Settlement Statement, it appears in an obscure place on the form. As a result, the loan officer can easily dismiss it with a "pay no attention to that figure" statement, even though the SRP may be an eventual cost to the borrower in the *thousands* of dollars.

BUT CAN'T I LATER REFINANCE MY SUB-PRIME MORTGAGE TO A LOWER, CONVENTIONAL RATE?

Yes, you may be able to. Wouldn't your loan officer like to make you a customer again?

But remember that each time you refinance, the new closing costs (if you don't pay them outright with cash) may be rolled into the loan. This will effectively reduce the equity you have in your home.

SHOULD I REFINANCE MY CONVENTIONAL MORTGAGE TO GET A LOWER RATE?

Whenever Ben Franklin needed to make a decision, he would take out a piece of paper and mark a large "T" on the sheet. On the left side of the "T" he would write all of the "pro" reasons—why he should go forward with the decision. On the right side of the "T" he would record all of the "con" reasons—why he should not go forward. Let's do the same thing:

PROs

o *Can reduce my monthly payment*
o *Can roll in other outstanding debts at higher interest rates*
o *Mortgage interest can be tax deductible*

CONs

o *Might be extending the term of the loan (back to the original fifteen or thirty full years). In other words, you could be spending less per month but be making payments for many additional months.*
o *Closing costs may be rolled back into the loan*

SHOULD I REFINANCE MY HOME IF THE DIFFERENTIAL IS LESS THAN TWO PERCENT?

Answer this question with another question: "Will I live in my home long enough after I refinance to save money?"

Here is an example:
o Thirty-year, fixed-rate loan of $100,000
o Current balance of $90,000
o Interest rate: eight percent
o Could re-finance to a thirty-year, fixed-rate loan of $90,000 at seven percent
o Closing costs: $1,200

The savings per month in switching to the lower-interest mortgage would be $127. Therefore, it would take you ten months to break even (divide the closing costs of $1,200 by the monthly savings of $127). Online mortgage calculators at Web sites such as www.bankrate.com can help you get the figures you need to make *your* decision.

If you are planning to move within the year, in this case, refinancing is probably not a good idea.

On the other hand, if you are going to stay in your home until the kids finish school or until you retire (and both events are a long way off), go ahead.

Chapter
Thirty-two

What is APR
(Annual Percentage Rate)?

T he Good Faith Estimate will have two percentage
rates listed on the form. One rate will be the actual
percentage of the loan. The other will be the APR (Annual
Percentage Rate).

What is the difference?

Well, to be sure, the APR will be the higher of the two
rates. But if you ask your loan officer he or she may just
shrug their shoulders and say, "Pay no attention to the APR,
this other is the rate you will pay."

Would you like to be one of the few people on the planet
who actually understands the meaning of APR?

Let's attempt to define the APR by way of two examples:

You need to borrow $1,000. You find someone to lend you
the money for a year at eight percent interest.

At the end of the year, you would repay the $1,000 plus
the $80 interest.

In this case, the APR and the interest rate would be the
same:

$80 / $1,000 = 8\%$

But, for our second example, let's assume that the lender collected a $25 service charge in advance (this would be similar to "closing costs"). In this case, you would receive $975 instead of $1,000.

You would then repay $105 instead of just $80 ($25 *plus* the $80).

The APR would be calculated as follows:

$105 / $975 = 10.77\%$

The APR was devised to give a more accurate picture of the real percentage rate for the loan, since it takes into account both components of a mortgage loan: interest rate *and* closing costs.

Therefore, in theory at least, you should be able to compare two loans with different interest rates and closing costs by looking at their respective APRs on the Truth-In-Lending Statements.

Chapter
Thirty-three

*Saving Money on
Closing Costs*

A lmost everything in the mortgage process is negotiable, especially closing costs. And you can negotiate
those costs not only with the lender but also with the seller.

For example, when negotiating the house's price with a
seller, you might ask the seller to pay *half* of your closing
costs. You just need to ask. You may be surprised at the response.

HOW TO NEGOTIATE THE BROKER'S COMMISSION

On a $75,000 loan, a one percent commission (or "origina-
tion fee") amounts to *$750*.

The same commission percentage on a $300,000 loan
equals *$3,000*.

Do you think a four-times-larger loan takes four times as
much of the broker's time?

Of course not! In fact, I'd bet that the larger loan with a
more creditworthy borrower was even *easier* to process.

Remember, it's *your* money! Look at the fee and calculate how many hours you had to work to pay for it. That will provide you the needed incentive to *negotiate*.

Chapter
Thirty-four

Do I Have to Pay Private Mortgage Insurance (PMI)?

It was common practice years ago that you could only purchase a house if you put twenty percent down on it.

In that way, the lender would be satisfied that the borrower had enough of a financial interest in the property to make sure it would be properly maintained. This would especially be the case if the house went to foreclosure and the bank would need to resell it. Even if the bank received only ninety percent of the mortgage amount on the sale, it would not likely lose money.

The down payment is the biggest stumbling block for many first-time house buyers. After all, their incomes may afford them the monthly cash flow and their rents may even approximate their monthly mortgage payment. The problem is that they don't have the thousands of dollars stashed away in savings. A twenty percent down payment on a $150,000 house is $30,000!

So, Private Mortgage Insurance (PMI) was created to make it easier to afford a house. By taking out a PMI policy, you may be able to move into a house with as little as five percent down. On a $150,000 house, a five percent down payment is a much more affordable sum—$7,500.

But please remember that PMI protects only the lender, not you. If you default on your mortgage payments, even with PMI, you are still likely to lose your house.

PMI premium payments are *not* tax deductible. After the initial advantage of allowing you to secure your own home, PMI offers you *no* benefits. And you will continue to pay premiums until you reach at least a twenty percent equity level. So you will want to stop paying for PMI just as soon as your lender will allow you.

But you have two factors working for you. Not only are you increasing the equity in your house by making regular payments on your mortgage principal, your house is also likely to be appreciating in value. Theoretically then, it is possible you could attain a twenty percent equity position in your home *without ever making a single mortgage payment*.

A lender may also offer you a creative way to avoid paying PMI. Let's say you were able to put 5 percent down. You could take out a mortgage for 80 percent of the value of the house, and then secure a second mortgage for the remaining 15 percent. Because the second mortgage would be considered of higher risk, the interest rate would be higher than that of the first mortgage. But this combination of a first mortgage subordinated by a second mortgage could result in a lower monthly payment than if you were simply to take out a single loan with a 95 percent loan-to-value *and* also pay PMI.

CANCELLATION OF PRIVATE MORTGAGE INSURANCE

The Homeowners Protection Act of 1998—which became effective in 1999—establishes rules for automatic termination and borrower cancellation of PMI on home mortgages. These protections apply to certain home mortgages signed on or after July 29, 1999 for the purchase, initial construction, or refinance of a single-family house. These protections *do not* apply to government-insured FHA or VA loans or to loans with lender-paid PMI.

For home mortgages signed *on or after* July 29, 1999, your PMI must—with certain exceptions—be terminated automatically when you reach twenty-two percent equity in your house based on the original property value, if your mortgage payments are current. Your PMI also can be canceled, when you request—with certain exceptions—when you reach twenty percent equity in your house based on the original property value, if your mortgage payments are current.

If you signed your mortgage *before* July 29, 1999, you can ask to have the PMI canceled once you exceed twenty percent equity in your house. But federal law does not require your lender or mortgage servicer to cancel the insurance.

On a $100,000 loan with ten percent down ($10,000), PMI might cost you $40 a month. If you can cancel the PMI, you can save $480 a year and many thousands of dollars over the loan. Check your annual escrow account statement or call your lender to find out exactly how much PMI is costing you each year.

ADDITIONAL PROVISIONS IN THE LAW

- o New borrowers covered by the law must be told—at closing and once a year—about PMI termination and cancellation.
- o Mortgage servicers must provide a telephone number for all their mortgage borrowers to call for information about termination and cancellation of PMI.
- o Even though the law's termination and cancellation rights do not cover loans that were signed

before July 29, 1999, or loans with lender-paid PMI signed on any date, lenders or mortgage servicers must tell borrowers about the termination or cancellation rights they may otherwise have under those loans (such as rights established by the contract or state law).

Chapter Thirty-five

Should I Put Down
More Than Twenty Percent?

T wenty percent is a magical figure. With that amount of down payment you can avoid paying Private Mortgage Insurance. But any additional dollars you put down don't have the same mystical quality.

If you invest more in your mortgage, you are probably only saving six to eight percent on that money. And if you look at the tax advantages you lose (not being able to deduct a higher mortgage interest expense on your taxes), the benefit is a lot less.

Moral: You would likely be further ahead by investing any additional cash elsewhere. For example, look into the benefits of beefing up your 410(k) balance or other retirement account.

Chapter
Thirty-six

Should I Try to Pay Off
My Mortgage Early?

T he answer may surprise you: **No.** But let's back up a minute.

There are two kinds of benefits you can get from paying off your mortgage balance:

o Psychological
o Financial

Let's look at the *psychological* benefits first.

With a zero balance on your mortgage, you have achieved a milestone few homeowners ever achieve. You may have been working your entire life to reach this goal. Rather than tying up hundreds or even thousands of dollars each month, you can now have the freedom to do what you have always wanted.

You may now have the cash flow to let you travel to visit your children or your grandchildren. Perhaps you could save for a few months and pay for a used RV or another vehicle—with cash. Or maybe you could even ease into retirement or semi-retirement.

Now let's look at the situation from a *financial* point of view:

It just doesn't make a lot of sense.

The money you used to pay off your mortgage could have been earning perhaps two or three times as much interest, or even more in another investment. What was the *opportunity cost* of that money?

Moral: If the best use of your money is to pay off your mortgage, then do it. But you are probably not looking at your options hard enough.

Chapter Thirty-seven

Should I Buy a Mortgage Life Insurance Policy?

How likely is it that your lender is also an insurance agent? More than likely your lender is acting as a middleman in offering you this policy. Beware: middlemen must also make a profit.

Mortgage life insurance policies tend to be *grossly overpriced* for the amount of insurance they offer.

What should you do?

After doing a comparison, you'll probably find low-cost, high-quality life insurance or long-term disability insurance to be a much better deal. Some unscrupulous lenders might even make add-ons such as credit life insurance, disability insurance, or home warranties a condition of the loan, possibly to increase the amount of their "kickbacks" from the vendors of such offerings. Don't fall for it!

Chapter Thirty-eight

Should I Co-Sign on a Loan?

M any times when one has a limited history of credit, the lender will ask the borrower if he or she could secure a co-signer for the loan. This is a person who will share the risk.

When you co-sign on a loan, that obligation can also appear on your credit report and be figured in to your debt-to-income ratio.

Before you sign on that dotted line with someone else, consider these two stories told to me by my customers:

CASE ONE

A long-haul truck driver had perfect credit for over twenty years. His son, in his early twenties, wanted to buy a pickup truck and a motorcycle.

"Sure, I'll sign with you," Dad said.

The truck driver would call his son from the road.

"Are you making those payments?"

"Sure," the son said. He lied.

Before long the father received a call from the attorney at the dealership. Apparently the son had not made a payment on either vehicle for over six months.

Settling the son's case of delinquent payments drove the father into bankruptcy.

Several months after the bankruptcy, the father went to purchase a pickup truck of his own. The salesperson told him, "We can finance you, but because of your credit history, the rate will be high."

My customer told me, "Right then and there I felt like kissing his feet. Everywhere else I had gone they took one look at my record, then treated me like dirt."

"I later told my son, 'Son, I'll always love you, but don't *ever* do that to me again!' "

CASE TWO

After years of searching, a young man finally found that special girl he wanted to make his wife. So he and his buddy went shopping for the perfect (meaning *expensive*) diamond engagement ring.

Because he didn't yet have credit established, he asked his buddy to sign with him when they found it at a jewelry store.

The young man then took the dazzling, sparkling ring to his potential bride-to-be.

"Will you marry me?" he proposed.

"No!" she replied.

No? That response was not part of his plan.

The young (and *stupid*) man was so upset that he flung the ring. It was never to be found.

Further, because the young man had neither the girl *nor* the ring, he didn't understand why he should have to pay for either.

Guess who had to make the monthly payments on the diamond ring?

If you guess the young man's buddy, you are wrong.

You see, in the buddy's household, it is his *wife* who pays the bills.

"So," the buddy's wife told me, "I'm paying for that diamond engagement ring that *I* never received when *he* proposed."

Moral of both stories: *You* must pay if your family member or friend doesn't when you co-sign on a loan. (And sometimes pay and pay and pay.)

Epilogue

After a year on the job as a senior loan officer, I checked my voicemail one day after coming back from lunch.

It was my previous employer.

"We want you to come back," the message said.

Halleluiah!

I had come to work for the mortgage company after I had lost my previous position at an electronic commerce network, software, and services provider. I detail that experience in my other book, *Real World Career Development: Strategies That Work*, Insight Publishing.

At the mortgage company, I had enjoyed advising my clients in financial matters but disliked the constant pressure from management to charge high fees. Why should one borrower pay twice or three times as much as the next one?

With great relief I returned to my previous employer. I worked there for over four years, until the dot com bubble burst.

I now train and speak, presenting seminars across the country for National Seminars Group and eBay.

Please note that the vast majority of mortgage lenders are honest and trustworthy. But a few are predatory and despicable. I wrote this book to help you tell the difference, because making a mistake could cost you thousands.

I'd love to share your mortgage experiences with you. Please send me an e-mail at eMint@att.net. If you have children who will be getting married or who have just completed college, this book could help them avoid some major, costly mistakes as they begin a new life. A copy of this book could make a thoughtful and appreciated wedding or graduation gift. Or if you are a banker or a Realtor, this book could bolster the knowledge and confidence of your understandably anxious clients who are first-time borrowers.

Additional copies can be ordered by telephone: 888-267-2665 (quantity discounts are available).

By helping to spread the word, you can help level the playing field in the most expensive game many of us will ever play.

And *you* can be a big part of my penance program.

Index

**Where to find a discussion of these common mortgage
terms in the book (*Don't* be intimidated!)**

The Top 10 Mortgage Mistakes People Make

1. Not knowing which mortgage fees you can - and cannot - negotiate.
2. Choosing and trusting the first loan officer you interview.
3. Using an interest-only loan primarily to qualify for a more expensive house. (You could be paying *forever* or, at the very least, you will pay more interest for a longer period of time.)
4. Thinking the interest rate is always the main thing. (What closing costs did you pay to get the rate?)
5. Not comparing the final fees listed on the closing documents to the up-front estimates (to avoid the lender "packing" the loan).
6. Not knowing if your mortgage has a pre-payment penalty - until it's too late.
7. Thinking that renting is always "just throwing money away." (At least in the short run, it can cost you thousands less to rent.)
8. Not knowing if you are paying a back-end yield spread or Service Release Premium (the lender has upsold you the rate).
9. Paying for mortgage life insurance, credit insurance or other expensive lender add-ons.
10. Paying hundreds of dollars to have a company set up a biweekly mortgage payment plan for you, something you can generally do yourself - for free.